BRITAIN IN OLD PHOTOGRAPHS

THE CHANGING EAST END
STEPNEY, BETHNAL GREEN
& POPLAR 1860–1960

The Town of Ramsgate pub, 62 Wapping High Street, by Wapping Old Stairs, *c.* 1960. This was a seventeenth-century pub which took its name in 1688 from the fishermen who came up the river from Ramsgate with their catch. Pirates were hanged at Execution Dock close to the pub's riverside gardens and local legend has it that Captain Kidd haunts the premises. The pub cellars were also used to house convicts awaiting transportation to Australia.

BRITAIN IN OLD PHOTOGRAPHS

THE CHANGING EAST END

STEPNEY, BETHNAL GREEN & POPLAR 1860–1960

ROSEMARY TAYLOR & CHRISTOPHER LLOYD

SUTTON PUBLISHING LIMITED

Sutton Publishing Limited
Phoenix Mill · Thrupp · Stroud
Gloucestershire · GL5 2BU

First published 1997

Reprinted 1998

Copyright © text: Rosemary Taylor and
Christopher Lloyd, 1997; © photographs:
London Borough of Tower Hamlets

British Library Cataloguing in Publication Data
A catalogue record for this book is available from the
British Library.

ISBN 0-7509-1574-9

Typeset in 10/12 Perpetua.
Typesetting and origination by
Sutton Publishing Limited.
Printed in Great Britain by
Ebenezer Baylis, Worcester.

Title page: The Aldgate and City Motors celebrating its thirty-fifth anniversary with the slogan '35 years and still working'. The company had its offices at 39 Commercial Road. Taking a break is the driver of the bus, George Richard Mersh.

Shadwell Basin, London Dock, with St Paul's Church to the rear, 1931. On the extreme right in the background are the premises of Meredith and Drew, biscuit manufacturers, who were at this time one of the largest local employers. In the distance can be seen the steeple of St Mary's, Cable Street.

CONTENTS

INTRODUCTION

O ur second book of old photographs illustrates the way of life in Stepney, Bethnal Green and Poplar before the three metropolitan boroughs in the East End of London merged to form the London Borough of Tower Hamlets thirty-two years ago. The name itself was not new: the Tower Hamlets were those villages whose duty it was to supply yeomen and guards to the Tower of London.

Stepney was the mother-parish, but Wapping, Ratcliffe, Limehouse, Bethnal Green, Mile End Old Town and Mile End New Town, Poplar, Bromley-by-Bow and Bow each had its own identity, and with an increasing population each in turn became an independent administrative area where business was conducted through the vestry and the vestrymen. In 1832 the name Tower Hamlets was given to the new parliamentary borough, but with a limited franchise,

Salter Street, Limehouse, 4 November 1932. The local greengrocer chats up a couple of prospective customers. Salter Street connected Limehouse Causeway with West India Dock Road, but with the widening of the latter, the street has partly disappeared.

granted to a favoured section of the male population, the majority of the residents of the East End could neither exercise their franchise nor aspire to a seat in parliament.

With the reorganisation of London in 1900 Stepney, Bethnal Green and Poplar took on their own identities, and each chose its own Coat of Arms, in which was reflected the history and character of each borough. Stepney's armorial bearings, granted in 1931, contained a ship symbolising the borough's seafaring associations, fire-tongs to represent St Dunstan, the patron saint of Stepney and of metal workers, the cross of St George, with the battlements and anchors in the crest representing the Tower of London, and the Port of London. The badge on the mayoral chain depicts St Dunstan's Church, the Tower of London and Blackwall Tunnel. Bethnal Green, the smallest of the three boroughs, had no Arms, but chose a Common Seal depicting the legend of the Blind Beggar of Bethnal Green. The story, although almost certainly legendary, probably had some basis in fact. As far back as 1690 it was used as a decoration for the Beadle's staff (see page 115) and was used on the official devices of the Council. The mace features the Blind Beggar and his daughter, as well as the parish church of St Matthew and the old Town Hall, in Church Row. The mayoral chain and badge, presented in 1902 by Henry Merceron, of Huguenot descent, has a fine onyx cameo, carved to illustrate the legend of the Blind Beggar. Incidentally, this chain is the one most favoured by the mayors of Tower Hamlets in recent years for use on official duties. Poplar too had no registered Coat of Arms, but adopted a Common Seal based on the badge designed for the Poplar Board of Works in 1855, comprising the seals of the parishes of Poplar, Bromley and Bow. Represented are the West India Dock Gate surmounted by the sailing ship *Hibbert* for Poplar, a monk representing the parish of Bromley St Leonard, where a Benedictine priory was founded in the tenth or eleventh century on the banks of the River Lea; and a bridge and two bows, to represent Bow and its association with Bow Bridge.

The history of the East End of London has been one of continuous change and growth as the area has developed through a constant movement of population. Maritime industries along the riverside attracted an ever-increasing workforce in search of a means of earning a livelihood. The influence of newcomers is reflected in the nature of businesses set up in the area by the Germans who developed the sugar and tobacco manufactories, the Scandinavians who monopolised the wood importing businesses, the Jewish refugees from Russia and Poland who set up shops and garment factories, the Chinese who came off the ships docking at Limehouse and the Irish who came to help build the docks and then stayed on to earn their living as dockers. The proliferation of churches, synagogues and more recently mosques reflects this more than any other outward sign of the presence of people who came in search of a refuge and adopted the East End as their own. A high proportion of the population lived on or below the poverty line and the overcrowded dwellings and insanitary living conditions were a constant source of anxiety to the more affluent West End of London. Religion and philanthropy combined in attempts to relieve the misery of the slum dwellers. The names of some the men and women who championed the cause of their less fortunate fellow beings deserve a mention: George Lansbury, Will Crooks, Canon Barnett, Dr Thomas Barnardo, Sylvia Pankhurst, Annie Besant, Annie Barnes, Mary Hughes, and Dr Hannah Billig are but a few.

Many of the East End's sons and daughters have gone on to achieve fame and fortune on stage, radio and screen, and it would not be out of place to spotlight the names of Bud Flanagan, Charles Coborn, Bernard Bresslaw, Lionel Bart, Angela Lansbury, the Beverley Sisters, Jack Warner and his sisters Doris and Elsie Waters, Warren Mitchell – the list is long and fascinating. Poets and writers too, such as Arthur Morrison, Israel Zangwill, Arnold Wesker, and the tragic poet Isaac Rosenberg, have risen from their humble backgrounds to shine in the literary world.

The three boroughs suffered more perhaps than any other part of London during the Blitz. Some 24,000 homes were destroyed or made uninhabitable, and the movement of people away from the area was inevitably accelerated. In 1939 the population of the three boroughs combined was 419,000, but this was reduced to 231,000 by 1951. Of the estimated 125,000 Jews in Stepney, barely a tenth of them remained, and the vacuum left by their departure was gradually filled by the newcomers to the area, the Bangladeshi, and to a lesser degree the Somali and others from Afro-Caribbean communities. Poplar seized the opportunity of rebuilding its devastated borough with a well-planned design, featured and celebrated during the Festival of Britain in 1951. But in other parts of the East End reconstruction was slow and sporadic. Sadly, of the dozens of churches destroyed or damaged, few were rebuilt and many have vanished without trace, so we have included a number of them in this new volume of photographs.

The riverside hamlets have lost much of their maritime character since the docks closed and wharves and warehouses ceased to function. For the first time in 500 years, the inhabitants of Stepney, Bethnal Green and Poplar no longer looked to the river for their livelihood. Industries too declined, and factories have closed or moved away, leaving only memories of sweatshops and low wages, marches and demonstrations, large families living in a single room, and a time when going on holiday meant a few weeks in the Kent countryside hop-picking. But other memories remain, just as evocative, when going down to Tunnel Gardens or Brunswick Pier, Victoria Park or Island Gardens was an adventure, when pennies were saved for the Country Holiday outing or the annual beano with the local pub, and who could forget the street parties celebrating the end of years of hardship with renewed hope for peace.

Poplar Hippodrome, East India Dock Road, on the corner of Stainsby Road, *c.* 1910. Built originally as a music hall, the Princes Theatre, it opened on 23 December 1905, but later became a cinema. The Hippodrome was badly damaged during the Second World War and was demolished in 1950.

TRAVELS THROUGH STEPNEY

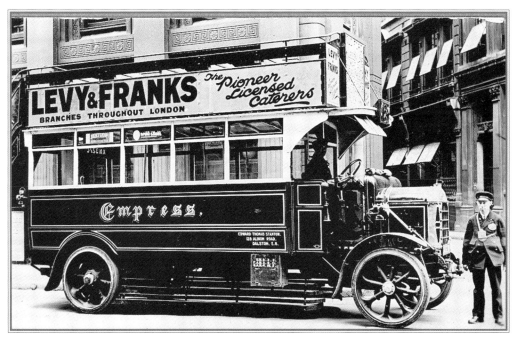

No. 8 bus operated by Empress Motors, 2 Corbridge Crescent, Bethnal Green. The conductor standing on the right was the founder of the company. Levy & Franks, advertised on the side as well as on the front panels of the bus, was a firm of caterers.

King George V unveiling the memorial at King Edward VII Park, Shadwell, 1922. Queen Mary can be seen on the left. The 7½-acre park was laid out on the site of the Shadwell Fish Market, one of Baroness Angela Burdett-Coutt's schemes to improve the lives of the working classes in the East End of London. In the background left is the George Peabody pub.

Empire Cinema, Mile End Road, 1938. The first building on this site was the Eagle public house, built in 1848, which later became Lusby's Music Hall. Destroyed by fire in 1884, it was rebuilt as the Paragon Theatre of Varieties. In 1912 the theatre was renamed the Mile End Empire and used as a cinema. In 1934 it was taken over by the ABC circuit, before being rebuilt in 1939. In 1963 the premiere of *Sparrows Can't Sing* was held at the ABC in the presence of Lord Snowdon. The film returned for a second charity performance in 1985. Sadly, it was to close within the next few years.

Popular Cinema, 516 Commercial Road, c. 1937. One of the earliest cinemas in East London, it opened in 1913 and seated an audience of 530. During the late 1930s the cinema was remodelled by George Coles. It closed on 13 June 1959, when the last pictures shown were *A Cry from the Streets* and *The Stooge*. The cinema was replaced, unromantically, by a petrol station. On the right is Ratcliffe Stairs Street.

The eastern end of Ropemakers Fields, c. 1900, looking eastwards towards Three Colts Street, Limehouse. Ropemakers Fields is now part of the Barley Mow Estate. The baker's handcart in the distance is in front of John Adam Siebert's wood-slatted bakery, at 93 Three Colts Street. Siebert was in business there from the 1880s to about 1908. The Ship and Lion pub, 65 Ropemakers Fields, is on the corner facing the bakery.

Mayfair Cinema, Brick Lane, 1939. Formerly the Brick Lane Palace which was demolished in 1935 and rebuilt, the Mayfair became the Odeon on 12 February 1950. In 1967 the Odeon closed but the theatre was to reopen in 1974 as the Naz, the first Asian cinema, owned by Mr Muktah Ahmed. The Naz Cinema closed in 1984, and it is now Café Naz.

Old Gravel Lane, 1910. The lane was used to transport sand for ballast from Kingsland to the wharves of Wapping, hence the name. It was changed to Wapping Lane in 1939.

The People's Palace, Mile End Road, 1936.
Destroyed by fire in 1931, it was rebuilt and
opened by George VI, the first public duty he
performed as King. The relief panels by Eric
Gill depict drama, music, fellowship, dance,
sport and recreation. The Hall was sold to
Queen Mary and Westfield College in 1954
and renamed the Queen's Building. The front
of the building was redesigned, the entrance
and steps removed, and the building reclad in
stone to harmonise with the main college
buildings.

Aerial photo of Queen Mary College, taken by Aero Pictorial Ltd. At first glance this appears to be a
model of the college buildings, but close inspection reveals an extraordinary view. In the background is
the burial ground of the Spanish and Portuguese Jews, closed in 1888; most of the gravestones are flat on
the ground. The graves, displaced by the college building extensions eastwards, have been sent to a new
site in Brentwood, Essex.

Arbour Square Garden, Stepney, *c.* 1920. Two rather severe-looking park-keepers guard the flowerbeds. To the east of the Square is Raine's Foundation School, built in 1913, now part of Tower Hamlets College. The early nineteenth-century terrace in the background survived demolition in 1973 but the terrace on the north side was demolished and replaced by Arbour House in 1937. The message on the reverse begins 'Dear E – are you still alive or dead, sorry we did not come to see you last Sunday....'

Thames Police Court, Arbour Square, *c.* 1906. In 1841 the Metropolitan Police rented land from the Mercers Company to build a police station and court. The court was opened here on 13 October 1842. It featured in the national news when William Morris was arrested here after protesting against the treatment of Free Speech Radicals, who had been brought before the magistrate for speaking in public at Dod Street in September 1887. Thames Police Court survived the Blitz but was hit by a V1 rocket in 1944, with 18 casualties. The Magistrates' Court has in recent years been moved to a modern building in the Bow Road.

Salmon Lane, *c.* 1910. Wyatt's furniture shop at no. 123 (on the extreme left), was run by Mrs Emily Wyatt from 1906 to 1940 and then by Albert Edward Wyatt until 1955.

Children in St Anne's Street, Limehouse, *c.* 1940. A small street off Commercial Road, almost opposite St Anne's Church, the area was cleared as part of Stepney's slum clearance and rebuilding programme. On the right is the even smaller turning into St Anne's Row, where in 1908 a new boys' school was opened by Fr Higley, the Catholic parish priest of Our Lady Immaculate, Limehouse.

Whitechapel Washhouses, situated between Goulston Street and Old Castle Street, 13 January 1938. The establishment suffered extensive damage during the Second World War, and was rebuilt after the war, offering, among other facilities, 1st and 2nd class Slipper Baths for men, but only 2nd class Slipper Baths for women. The Advance Laundries Ltd were started at 40–42 Oxford Street in around 1930 and by 1938 had several outlets including Manor Park Laundry, where this van travelled from.

This Dennis street watering vehicle no. 1 was part of a fleet of transport used by the Public Cleansing Department of the Stepney Metropolitan Borough, 1937.

The tow-path by Cricketer's Bridge, Bethnal Green, 1937. The bridge over the Regent's Canal, also known as Old Ford Road Bridge, takes its name from the nearby Royal Cricketer public house. The Regent's Canal was opened on 1 August 1820 and runs from Paddington to Limehouse, forming the western border of Victoria Park. The canal provided a convenient means of transporting building materials from the Regent's Canal Dock in Limehouse to the new communities of north London in the nineteenth century. Horses continued to be used for towing barges until 1956 and were then replaced by diesel tugs.

ALONG THE RIVERFRONT

The Wapping Entrance to the London Docks and Western Dock, designed by the engineer John Rennie and built in 1801. In 1805 the lock was 40 ft wide and 170 ft long with a depth of 23 ft, but by the 1930s the locks had become inadequate for the large ocean-going vessels of the day. From the late 1960s the locks and the docks were filled in. The Pierhead houses on the right were designed by Daniel Alexander and built between 1811 and 1813. On the extreme left is The Town of Ramsgate pub by Wapping Old Stairs.

W. Paros Ltd, the India rubber waste stores at 242–4 Cable Street, went up in flames on 17 July 1935. This picture was taken at 12.30 p.m. from the London Dock.

Sailing ships in the Regent's Canal. This is one of a series of photographs taken in 1905 of London's docks. The side of the wharf house bears the name of the canal.

Industry on the River Thames. Noxious black smoke belched from the chimneys of factories such as Burrell's Colour Works, Millwall Leadworks, McDougall's Flour Mill and Hooper's Telegraph and India Rubber Works, all on the north bank of the river on the Isle of Dogs.

Shipping in the South West India Dock in the 1870s. Originally built in 1805 as the City Canal, it was acquired by the West India Dock Company and enlarged between 1866 and 1870, with new warehouses on the south side.

John Stewart's Blackwall Ironworks on the Isle of Dogs, *c.* 1863. John Stewart's yard was situated in Manchester Road, and was closed in 1924 when the premises were taken over by the PLA for the South West India Dock extension, opposite Glen Terrace.

The *Faraday*, an under-sea cable-laying ship. The vessel was built in 1874 and was a frequent visitor to the West India Docks.

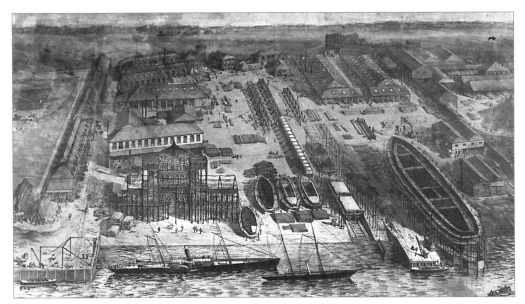

Westwood, Baillie and Co., 1880, from a coloured lithograph by R. Newberry. Joseph Westwood worked for Thames Iron Works before setting up his own shipbuilding business in 1850 with his colleagues Baillie and Campbell. They moved on to the production of wrought iron and the firm was involved all over the world in the construction of railway bridges. Westwood died in 1883, leaving a fortune of £29,000.

The Guinness berth at London Docks, 1955. The *Corvus*, built in 1947, was registered in Bergen, Norway. It is moored at no. 19 Eastern Dock. The new shed nearby was the first of its type to use pre-stressed concrete. The aluminium alloy sheeting greatly reduced maintenance costs and enabled the latest mechanical equipment to be used.

The Grapes public house, *c.* 1935. One of the oldest pubs in the East End, there has been a pub on this site since the sixteenth century, although the building dates from the late eighteenth century, with the present façade dating from the nineteenth. There is an excellent view of the river from the balcony window. On the right is the Harbour Master's house.

Millwall Ironworks and Shipbuilding Company, *c.* 1863. The yard was established in 1835 by William Fairbairn, then taken over in the 1850s by John Scott Russell and it was here that Brunel's ship the SS *Great Eastern* was built and launched. The yard subsequently passed into the hands of C.J. Mare, and was renamed Millwall Ironworks and Shipbuilding Company.

Baron Kato, a Japanese minister, on a visit to Orchard Place on 18 March 1895. He is inspecting the progress of the battleship *Fuji*, under construction at Thames Iron Works.

The shipbuilding yard of Messrs James Ash & Co. in Cubitt Town, *c.* 1863. James Ash was formerly in the employ of C.J. Mare & Company and later worked for the Thames Iron Works and Shipbuilding Co. Around 1862 he set up his own business on the Isle of Dogs, in Manchester Road, close to Pier Street.

James Ash and Co., shipbuilders, at Manchester Road, Cubitt Town, on the Isle of Dogs, *c.* 1863.

Samuda's Shipbuilding Yard, *c.* 1863. Joseph and Jacob Samuda set up their engine building yard at Blackwall in 1832, and by 1842 they had gone into shipbuilding. The firm built iron steamships for the Royal Navy as well as passenger ships. Joseph Samuda died in 1885, and the yard closed in 1893.

The boardroom at the offices of the Thames Ironworks, Orchard Yard, 1900. On the walls is a fascinating display of models of ships that had been built at the yard, including HMS *Warrior*, the first iron battleship, built in 1859.

Torpedo boat no. 80, the fastest vessel in Her Majesty's Navy, March 1887. Built by Yarrow and Co., the vessel was 135 ft long, with a beam of 14 ft. It could maintain a speed of 23 knots for two hours, carrying 15 tons. Yarrow's on the Isle of Dogs was the first shipyard to manufacture torpedo boats.

Transit shed at Millwall Dock, 1965. This view of the new development shows part of C shed and C2 shed at rear. The ship is the *Suecia*. The River Thames can be seen in the distance and St Anne's Church steeple is just visible. All of this has now been replaced by the new development around the Marsh Wall area.

Blackwall station, looking east along the track. Aspen Way, a new road leading towards the offices of Reuter's International News Agency, follows the approximate line of the railway.

Brunswick Wharf, 1920, showing the entrance to the East India Dock Export Basin. This is a fine view of Blackwall railway station, which opened in 1840 and closed in 1926, shortly after the General Strike. In the distance the Brunswick Tavern can just be seen.

The River Thames below Blackwall, February 1895. The river was frozen for several weeks, an event we are not likely to witness again. The construction of Old London Bridge was such that it impeded the flow of the river, allowing the surface to freeze. This photograph was taken eight months after the opening of Tower Bridge.

GLIMPSES OF BETHNAL GREEN

Bethnal Green Pearly Kings and Queens collecting for a charity appeal on behalf of the City of London Hospital, Victoria Park, c. 1914. Now known as the London Chest Hospital, the City of London Hospital for Diseases of the Heart and Lungs was founded in 1848 in Liverpool Street, and moved to its present site in Approach Road in 1851.

THE CHILDRENS' HOSPITAL, HACKNEY ROAD.

This postcard of the Children's Hospital, Hackney Road, Bethnal Green, is dated 24 August 1905. Built in 1903, the hospital was renamed the Queen's Hospital for Children in 1907 and finally the Queen Elizabeth Hospital for Children in 1942, when it was amalgamated with the Children's Hospital, founded in Shadwell in 1867 by Nathaniel Heckford and his wife Sarah (née Goff). Married in 1867, Nathaniel was able to use Sarah's money to realise his dream, but he died in 1871.

Brick Lane north from Virginia Road, looking towards Bethnal Green Road, Sunday 3 January 1932. The Sunday markets in the Brick Lane area have not lost their appeal, and in recent years have spilled over into neighbouring streets, as far as Vallance Road to the east.

Quite a collection of people, including a policeman, pose for the photographer outside the Flowerpot public house, 120 Bethnal Green Road, on the corner of Brick Lane, proprietor E. Wallis. The pub has a splendid set of three decorative wrought-iron lamps. This card was posted on 10 September 1908.

A London Passenger Transport RTL Leyland, a type first built in 1948, on the 106 route between Stoke Newington and Becontree. This picture was taken in about 1952 in the East India Dock Road, looking towards Limehouse and St Anne's Church.

Victoria Park Baptist Church in Grove Road, *c.* 1905. The spire in the distance is that of St Barnabas Church, at the corner of Roman Road and Grove Road. The church lost its spire when it was damaged during the Second World War. Travelling towards the camera is a horse-drawn tram.

Nos 180 to 200 Roman Road, prior to demolition, August 1952. No. 180 was the Angel and Crown pub which moved to 170 Roman Road. No. 182 was the premises of Kovler and Greenwood, furniture manufacturers, and no. 188 was BB Radio and Television Co.

The Mayor of Bethnal Green takes the salute at the march-past of the borough's Peace Parade beside Bethnal Green Library, 11 November 1951. The band of the Salvation Army provided the music and nurses from the Bethnal Green Hospital, local units of the British Legion, the Civil Defence Corps, the St John Ambulance Brigade and the Women's Voluntary Service participated. By 1957 this parade was considerably reduced in size.

Carnival in Bethnal Green, 1958. Lorry no. 15 from the Digby Street depot advertises the pleasures of reading, on behalf of the Bethnal Green Library.

Entrance to Meath Gardens, Bethnal Green, September 1954. This concrete Gothic arch is the entrance to what was Victoria Park Cemetery, opened in 1845. The cemetery specialised in cheap burials for children and many were from Huguenot families. The cemetery was eventually closed to burials and in 1894 the nine acres were converted into a public garden by the Metropolitan Gardens Association. On 31 July 1996 a commemorative plaque was restored to the site where a eucalyptus tree had been planted in 1988 to honour the Aboriginal Australian cricketer, King Cole. King Cole died on 21 June 1868 during a tour of the first Australian cricket team to visit England, and was buried in a pauper's grave.

CHILDHOOD DAYS

Children enjoying a paddle in Victoria Park's boating lake, c. 1920. The lakes in the park attracted bathers from the outset. The boating lake was opened in 1846, and East Enders immediately began to use it for their ablutions. A bathing lake was constructed in 1847 and strict regulations were applied to control the thousands of men and boys who queued from 5 a.m. for their early morning dip.

Children in Coventry Ward at Mildmay Mission Hospital, Bethnal Green, *c.* 1900. The hospital was built as a memorial to the Revd William Pennefather. Miss Coventry, a founder of the Order of Deaconesses at Mildmay, planted a plane tree in the courtyard when the building was opened in 1892. The tree is still there, but Coventry Ward was converted in 1987 into a hospice for people terminally ill with Aids, and renamed the Elizabeth Unit.

Children posing patiently for the photographer in Edward Street, *c.* 1918. Note that some of them are barefoot. The doorway to the left has an interesting bow window, as well as a bootscraper.

Frying Pan Alley in Spitalfields, *c.* 1912. The girl on the left in a dark dress is well dressed and wears a fine pair of boots, as do all the other children with the exception of the boy on the extreme left, who just manages to sneak into the picture.

Education at the London Chinese Evangelical Mission, 33 Pennyfields, 1936. The Baptist Mission was founded in May 1925 and the Mission House was opened on 24 January 1934, in the premises formerly occupied by the Scandinavian Reading Rooms (1900–32). The resident missionaries were Mr and Mrs Sing Nuer Sheng. The Mission closed when the building was damaged by enemy action in 1941 and was succeeded in 1942 by the Ho Ling Restaurant, followed by the Chinese Seamen's Club from about 1943 to 1956. Most of the street was demolished in the early 1960s.

Evacuees walking down the East India Dock Road towards Poplar Station, 1939. The building in the background is King George's Hall, which stood next door to Poplar Methodist Mission.

Children lining up in Hanbury Street for a farthing breakfast, handed out by the Salvation Army. The picture was one of many taken to generate funds for the philanthropic work carried out by the missions. Unusually for this period, all these children are well shod, some with very shiny boots indeed.

No. 2 Willow Row, Limehouse, 19 October 1931. No. 2 was on the corner of Brightlingsea Place, with Willow Row on the left. The buildings in the distance to the south are Brightlingsea Buildings, now demolished, where Clement Attlee, later Prime Minister, rented four good rooms for 8s 6d a week from 1911 to 1912.

Childhood games in Whitechapel, 1915, from the collection of the Revd Cecil Cohen. A curate of St Mary's, Whitechapel, from 1912 to 1915, Father Cohen took a number of photographs of local children which he used for his charity appeals.

Children at Whitechapel, *c*. 1915. This picture comes from a series of scenes taken by the Whitechapel Mission; intended to stir the social conscience of the middle classes, they depicted the dire poverty of the area at the turn of the century. Beautifully photographed by the Revd Cecil Cohen, these pictures have made a valuable contribution to social history.

The children of Bethnal Green receive gift parcels from Canada on 24 February 1949. The Mayor, Cllr George Hemsley, distributed the parcels, assisted by Mrs Irene Rosen of the WVS. The parcels each contained salmon, spam, peaches, drinking chocolate, biscuits, sweets, chewing gum, chocolate and a book.

Drinking fountain at the corner of Jubilee Street and Mile End Road, Stepney, *c.* 1900. To the extreme right can be seen the hands of a shoeshine boy. The Vintner's Almshouses in the background, to the right of James Avila, pawnbroker, were established here in 1676, after the fire of London, and rebuilt in 1802. The almshouses were built to provide homes for twelve women.

Children enjoying their playtime in the Clifton Street playground, which was opened in 1936. This is a view looking south-east; St Saviour's Church can be seen in the background. Note the children and dogs at the drinking fountain in the foreground.

Children pose happily for the cameraman in the park in 1954, under the watchful eye of the park-keeper. The scene is the Abbott Road playground, which was between Dee Street and Ettrick Street in Poplar.

Puppies for sale in Club Row, Bethnal Green, 1953. Just about anything could be bought at the Sunday markets in the streets around Brick Lane. Club Row has now ceased to be part of the Sunday market area.

THE TIMES OF OUR LIVES

'Ole Bill', the LGOC's (Local Government) bus, famous during the First World War, takes part in the fancy dress parade and street collection for Poplar's children in the Carnival held on Sunday 21 July 1925.

The Russian Vapour Baths at 86 Brick Lane, *c.* 1910. These Jewish ritual baths were situated opposite the Machzike Hadass, the Great Synagogue on the corner of Fournier Street and Brick Lane. They were run by Rabbi Benjamin Schevzik and the Friday afternoon visit to Schevzik's baths by orthodox Jews became part of an East End tradition, which continued until the beginning of the Second World War, when the baths were closed following a fire.

This scene, entitled 'The Sellers In Whitechapel', by the Whitechapel Mission, was used as part of a fund-raising appeal for the work of the mission in Three Colts Lane, off Cambridge Heath Road.

Poplar Workhouse, on Poplar High Street, 1905. This is the kitchen where the staff are busy preparing a meal for the inmates. The workhouse building was demolished in 1959 and Tower Hamlets College built an extension over part of the site. However, the remainder of the site of the workhouse is still open space.

Girls dancing in the open air in Poplar Park in 1919; this was one of the many celebrations held to mark the peace.

The Presbyterian Settlement of St Paul's in Millwall, 1899. An inscription on the reverse reads 'The first lot of girls to help the club here every Tuesday night'. All but one of the girls worked at Morton's Factory, where all manner of foodstuffs were preserved and packaged. The factory was one of the largest employers of women on the Isle of Dogs.

The opening of the LCC's Maternity Centre in Cornwall Avenue, Bethnal Green, 29 May 1922. The opening ceremony was performed by the Mayor of Bethnal Green, Cllr J.J. Vaughan. In 1965 the centre was taken over by Tower Hamlets and it changed from a maternity clinic to a training centre for handicapped children, and later a social services department. The building is now used as a mosque.

The Rising Sun public house on the corner of Globe Road and Green Street (now Roman Road), Bethnal Green, *c.* 1910. The view is south down Globe Road towards Stepney Green station. The spire of St Peter's, Mile End, can be seen in the distance. The shop at no. 237 on the extreme right belonged to Walter Henry Cole, grocer.

The annual outing from the Rising Sun public house, Bethnal Green, 1890. The all-male group of day-trippers pose for their picture in Grove Road before setting off. The annual outing was an eagerly awaited event and most East End pubs planned these occasions for their regulars.

Families in high spirits getting ready for their outing to Chessington Zoo from the Collingwood Estate, Cambridge Heath Road, 10 July 1952.

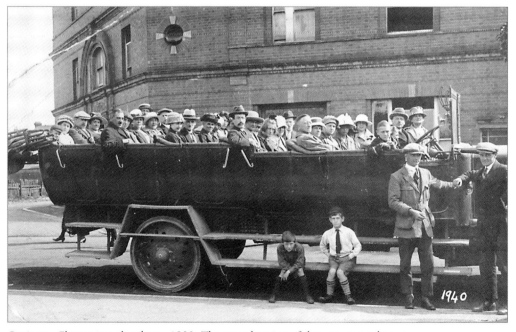

Outing to Clacton in a charabanc, 1920. The exact location of this view is not known.

Demonstration in Cambridge Heath Road, Bethnal Green, *c*. 1930. The banner across the side of the lorry reads: 'South West Bethnal Green Labour Party, disaffiliated but still going strong.' The banner to the left of the lorry is that of the Transport & General Workers Union and on the right is the banner of the Union of Corporation Workers, which features the Burdett-Coutts drinking fountain in Victoria Park.

Outside the premises of A. & H. Melzer Ltd, wholesale boot and shoe makers, 261 Cambridge Heath Road. The Metropolitan Workingmen's Club and Institute was at no. 265. The lorry bears the legend 'Workers of the World Unite, Agitate and Make a Fight'. The large man on the right features in both this view and the one above, indicating that these two lorries were part of the same demonstration.

East India Dock Gates, *c.* 1910. A wild animal is being transported from the docks down the East India Dock Road, probably bound for the Zoological Gardens, or else being taken to Jamrach's Wild Animal Shop on the Highway. The dock gates and imposing arch were removed and rebuilt in about 1913 during a road widening scheme and finally demolished during the building of the second Blackwall Tunnel, opened in 1967.

Pub outing from The Conqueror, Bethnal Green, *c.* 1905. The man second from the left inside the coach is Basil Saunders, grandfather of Peter Saunders, who kindly donated this picture to the library.

Staff of the Munitions Foundry of the Commercial Gas Company, 1915–17. The government took over factories for the production of military equipment in wartime. Notice the shoes of the workforce: they wore clogs with leather flaps which wrapped around the ankles to prevent accidental contact with molten metal.

Making a Coronation cake, 1937. The Commercial Gas Company held a weekly cookery demonstration at the Gas Co-partnership Institute in East India Dock Road. Modern gas appliances are prominently displayed on the stage. The building is now Pope John House and is used by Holy Family School as a school hall and also as a community centre for, among other things, a Chinese Lunch Club.

May Day Procession down the Mile End Road, 1938, passing Wickhams Department Stores. Leading the way is Mr Daniel Frankel, MP for Mile End (1935–45). Dan Frankel was born in Mile End in 1900 and followed his father in the tailoring profession. He was a Labour councillor in Stepney and Mayor of Stepney in 1929. He died in 1988.

Mrs Sarah Abbott being presented with a handmade quilt by Cllr H.E. Tate, Deputy Mayor of Bethnal Green, on 17 October 1950. The quilt was one of the many gifts sent to Bethnal Green by the people of Timaru, New Zealand.

This photograph from the family album of Mrs Martha Page of Wapping recalls the annual hop-picking trip to Yelding. Families planned their trip for months beforehand, collecting and storing items in their 'hopping box' – old pots and pans, knives and forks, curtains, etc. Everything they would need during their stay of up to eight weeks had to be packed and taken down.

An East End couple on their annual hopping trip. For many East End families, 'hopping' was the only holiday break they had. Women and children usually went hopping, with the men joining their families at weekends.

Jewish wedding, *c.* 1930. These two photographs were discovered in a house in Woodseer Street and presented to Bancroft Library. The photographer was L. & J. Suss, of 25 Whitechapel Road. The establishment closed in 1983.

Jewish wedding couple, *c.* 1930. By the same photographer, this picture was found with the picture above, and probably shows the same family. Woodseer Street is a turning off Brick Lane, east side, between Hanbury Street and Buxton Street.

The New Yiddish Theatre Company at Adler Hall, Adler Street, 1946. Pictured here are the cast of *The Merchant of Venice*, some of whom have been identified. Standing at the rear: Philo Hauser, -?-, A. Meisels, David Segal, -?-, Meta Segal, -?-, Anna Tzelniker, -?-, Meier Tzelniker, Max Baum, -?-, Freda Tentler, Leon Blumenson. Kneeling: Joseph Sherman, Ida Sherman, -?-, Julian Gold.

Latimer Chapel ladies enjoying a party. The picture is undated, but the chapel was destroyed in the Second World War and rebuilt in the 1950s, so this picture dates from about 1930.

William Whiffin took this photograph of ladies having their feet attended to at the Chiropodist Clinic in Poplar Methodist Mission. Known locally as Lax's Church, the Methodist Mission was on the corner of Woodstock Terrace and East India Dock Road.

Limehouse Pier, *c.* 1910–14. The lighters on the barge bed probably belonged to the Dundee, Perth & London Shipping Co. which built Dundee Wharf in 1899–1901. The River Plate Wharf dates from 1911, and was later part of Dundee Wharf. The pub on the right was the Horns and Chequers.

A group of young men enjoy a musical interlude at the Chinese Mission, 92 West India Dock Road, 1936. The Mission was one of several set up in the area in the 1920s and '30s. The building was demolished, along with most of the south side of the road, when the West India Dock Road was widened in 1989–90.

Women workers at the Globe Rope Works of Hawkins & Tipson Ltd, East Ferry Road, Millwall, *c.* 1910. The women are flanked by two men supervisors, who display samples of rope made. The firm closed in 1971 and in the 1980s the site was cleared to make way for the Docklands Light Railway, Mudchute station.

Display of rope at the Globe Rope Works of Hawkins & Tipson Ltd, Millwall. Established in 1881, the company produced a variety of ropes, including the extra-strong 'Hercules'. Rope was made from hemp or manila fibre, which was spun into yarn and then twisted and retwisted to form the required thickness. This work was done in the rope-walks, which had rails carrying the ropemaking machines. One set of these rails was preserved when the area was landscaped in the 1980s.

Mrs Robinson of Bethnal Green, *c.* 1900. She was paid 1*s* per mattress as a homeworker, stuffing straw into mattress covers.

Roman coffin excavated in Old Ford, Bow, on 22 May 1868. The slightly coped lid, broken into several parts, is not shown. This is only one of several coffins and skeletal remains found in the area during the construction of the railway. Recently, while laying cables for the Cable TV company, workmen found further remains in the Armagh Road area.

The 94th London Company, Boys' Brigade, with their Captain, Mr H.V. Lovejoy, outside the Bruce Road Congregational Church, Bromley-by-Bow, 1904. The photographer was Charles E. Long of 60 Bow Road. The church was wrecked in an air raid in 1940, but was rebuilt and reopened on 15 March 1958. It is now a thriving community centre, combining arts and crafts and care in the community.

HIGHWAYS, BYWAYS AND BRIDGES

The view from the west side of Mile End Road looking towards La Bohème Cinema, 1936. The cinema was later renamed the Vogue. The pub on the right is the Royal Hotel, licencee William A. Jackman. To the left of the cinema is a dancing hall, proprietors Moss and Zinkin. Bow Infirmary, now St Clement's, can be seen in the distance.

The corner of Whitechapel High Street and Commercial Road at the junction of Leman Street, Gardiner's Corner, 1906. In the distance is the spire of St Mary's Church, Whitechapel, damaged during the Second World War and finally destroyed when lightning struck the spire in July 1945, splitting it in two.

The distinctive clock tower of Gardiner's clothing store, *c.* 1900; this is the view eastwards down Commercial Road with a sign in lights advertising Gardiner's Summer Sale. The photographer is S. Eisner & Son. Gardiner's was destroyed by fire in May 1972 and the site is now occupied by Lloyd's Bank building.

Gardiner's Corner, the Scotch House, 1 to 5 Commercial Road, 1930. No. 7 was Nevill's Turkish Baths Ltd. In the foreground is the No. 67 tram to Barking.

Stepney Bridge in Commercial Road, constructed by Alfred Langley in 1875. Langley was an engineer for the Midland Railway. The family residence, Langley House in East India Dock Road, was demolished in May 1997, although a gate-post with the name Langley Place has survived, adjacent to the old NatWest Bank building.

Branch Road, 1955, the view looking northwards to Commercial Road. The railway bridge visible through the arch is the British Rail to Stepney East station, now named Limehouse on the Docklands Light Railway. Also seen through the arch is a police box. In the left foreground is a toll-post, which has survived to the present day.

Branch Road, 1955, looking south from Commercial Road through the railway bridge built to carry the Blackwall Railway, now refurbished for the Docklands Light Railway. The building seen on the left through the arch is the Seamen's Mission.

La Bohème Cinema on Mile End Road, 1931, viewed from Grove Road looking towards Burdett Road. It is difficult now to reconcile this view with the modern Mile End/Grove Road junction, as Grove Road was considerably widened and aligned with Burdett Road, in the process of which La Bohème, by that time renamed the Vogue, was demolished. However, the rear wall which held the screen is still standing and is just visible.

The official opening of Blackwall Tunnel, 22 May 1897. The tunnel was opened by the Prince of Wales, later Edward VII, on behalf of Queen Victoria. The Prince was accompanied by Princess Alexandra. Here we see the royal carriage entering the tunnel on the Blackwall side. The tunnel took five years to build, and over 600 men were employed in its construction, with the loss of nine lives. Running a total length of 4,460 ft, of which 1,220 ft is under the River Thames, the tunnel was considered a feat of modern engineering. The work was carried out by Pearsons to the plan of A.R. Binnie.

A panoramic view of the Blackwall Tunnel approach, looking south, 1967. In the background is the Charringtons Oil Depot at Blackwall. This photograph was taken at the time of the completion of the second tunnel, to the east of the original.

The premises of Ward Brothers at 329 Mile End Road, June 1951. The firm is still in business. Further along the road, no. 337 was Cyril Savino's cafe while no. 339 housed the Co-operative Wholesale Society. Wards' is all that remains of the many commercial establishments along this section of the road, most of which have given way to the ever-expanding premises of Queen Mary and Westfield College.

Nos 240–250 Mile End Road, opposite Stepney Green station, 6 August 1953. The estate agents had closed down, but at no. 244 was the café run by G. Pallicaros.

Tredegar House, Bow Road, *c.* 1910. Built on land owned by Lord Tredegar, the house was occupied by Joseph Westwood, shipbuilder, and later became the Training School for Probationary Nurses of the London Hospital. Nurse Edith Cavell, who was accused of spying and executed by the Germans in Belgium in June 1915, did her medical training here. The Bow Road is a continuation of the Mile End Road and is the main highway from Aldgate to Stratford.

Roadway into Spurlings Wharf over the Regent's Canal, 1933. The stones used in making the wall of the bridge were salvaged from Old London Bridge and Old Aldgate.

Burdett Road, 1908. The road was built in the 1860s to serve as a route northwards from Poplar to Victoria Park. Originally called Victoria Road, it was renamed Burdett Road in honour of Baroness Angela Burdett-Coutts. In the distance is the Tabernacle, while the establishment of J. Masters, watchmaker, is at no. 55 on the right.

The Earl of Zetland pub at the corner of Baggally Street, no. 137 Burdett Road. Frederick Voller was the licensee between 1908 and 1911.

Burdett Road, looking north, at the corner of Thomas Street (now Road). The Truman's pub on the right has the date 1862. Although the name of the pub is not evident, the Lovat Arms is now on this site. The photographer has managed to capture a great deal of movement in this view. There is a man on a ladder washing the window, a young girl crosses the road, while another dodges the carriages.

The Salisbury Arms, 111 Burdett Road, at the junction with Eric Street, 1908. The pub dispensed Barclay, Perkins Ales from the Anchor Brewery at Southwark. Following a merger with Courage in 1955, the brewery closed in 1958. In the distance on the right is the fire station.

This view is looking south from Burdett Road to a major junction in Limehouse, with the East India Dock Road on the left, West India Dock Road due south and Commercial Road to the right, 21 March 1952. Travellers found accommodation in the Sailor's Palace, seen in the centre background, and the Great Eastern Hotel on the left.

The view north from the Great Eastern Hotel and up Burdett Road, 1952. Barclays Bank, 534 Commercial Road, is now a pizza takeaway, and next door Boots the chemist is now Nash Chemists. The overhead cables which powered the trolley-buses produced lower air pollution levels than the diesel-fuelled buses that succeeded them in the 1960s.

Looking east to the new Canning Town Bridge connecting Poplar and West Ham which replaced the old Iron Bridge, photographed in 1933. The bridge opened unofficially in December 1932.

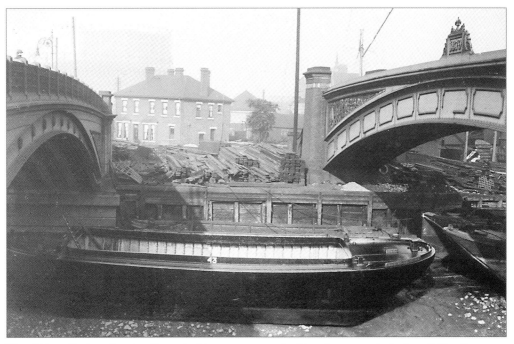

The old Iron Bridge, Canning Town, looking west across the River Lea towards the Iron Bridge Tavern, *c.* 1930. On the right is the gas and water bridge built in 1870.

The old Iron Bridge, Canning Town, looking eastwards, *c*. 1930, with the no. 67 tram to Barking. The bridge was built in 1896 by Thames Iron Works at Orchard Yard, and was replaced by a new bridge in 1932.

The old Iron Bridge, Canning Town. It was built in 1896 by Thames Iron Works. This 1930s view is eastwards.

PAST TIMES IN POPLAR

The Missions to Seamen Institute, East India Dock Road and Hale Street, undated. The building, previously owned by the Gas Co-partnership, was acquired by St Mary and St Joseph's Catholic parish and re-named Pope John House. It was converted into a club and social centre in the 1960s.

Flanked by the two establishments of Lewis Lewis & Co., drapers, this is the Lifeboat public house at 283 East India Dock Road (north side), on the corner of St Leonard's Road, 1906. In 1911 the licensee of the pub was William Henry Emmens. Unfortunately, all this was swept away in the building of the northern approach to the second Blackwall Tunnel.

St Leonard's Road, 1904, viewed from East India Dock Road. The landlord of the pub on the left at no. 279, later to become the Sir John Franklin, was Louis Wheatley. On the right is Lewis Lewis & Co.

This Charles Martin postcard shows Bow Chambers, Bow Road, looking north-west from St Mary's Church, *c.* 1910. The building has survived remarkably unchanged. To the right of the building at no. 199 is Francis Marsland, printers, then Durham Brothers, ironfounders, Sheridan Knowles & Co., and at no. 209 Bow Branch post office. To the extreme right is Geo. Betts, harness maker.

The no. 108A bus in St Leonard's Street, Bromley-by-Bow, 1956. The view is northwards towards the Recreation Grounds and Old Palace School. No. 32 on the extreme left was SB Panels Ltd, veneers and plywood manufacturers. The street leading off to the left is Grace Place. No. 28 is Thomas Childs, tobacconists.

Men and women at Poplar Baths, 1934. Whitechapel Baths (*see* page 135) pre-dated the first Baths and Wash-houses Act, and Poplar Baths was the first to be opened following the first Act of Parliament enabling authorities to establish them. They were originally built for bathing and laundry, at a time when most houses did not have bathrooms or indoor plumbing.

A group of council officials at the opening of the Violet Road open air swimming baths, 9 May 1921. The baths cost £6,000 and were designed by the borough architect Harley Heckford. George Lansbury (*see* page 127) can be seen behind the lifebuoy. In the background is the Church of All Hallows, which stands on the junction of Blackthorn Street and Devon's Road, Bromley-by-Bow.

Floods at Orchard Place, 7 January 1928. This picture was taken at noon and shows the residents of Orchard Place being rescued from their flooded homes. Much of the Isle of Dogs was also flooded as a result of a tidal surge, and the waters entered the Blackwall Tunnel. Shortly afterwards, the community at Orchard Place were compulsorily rehoused in Canning Town and Poplar. The Thames Barrier, built in 1973–82, now prevents any more flooding.

A funeral cortège passes Crang & Boreham, estate agents, 78 East India Dock Road, *c.* 1935. This view is from the north side of the road looking across to Oriental Street.

Traffic chaos in Cotton Street at the corner of East India Dock Road, where a lorry appears to have shed its load, *c.* 1930. The pub on the left is the Eagle Tavern at 182 East India Dock Road; it was demolished by a V2 on 7 March 1945 and the landlady, Mrs Mary Story, was killed. No. 184 is the East and West End Laundry Company.

An adult evening class on 'Homing Pigeons' discusses the merits of pigeon racing at the Stepney Men's Institute in Gill Street, Limehouse. The instructor is Mr Edgar Rickards.

DOCK LIFE, DOCK STRIFE

Free Trade Wharf, The Highway, Shadwell 1934, built by the East India Company in 1796 to store salt-petre. The gateway still stands and leads to the warehouses, now converted into offices.

Police officers at the London and St Katharine's Docks, 1891. They are wearing the helmet badge of the London and India Dock Company Police.

Dock strike, July 1923. Here the demonstrators enter East India Dock Road from Cotton Street. The film *The Sky Pilot*, advertised on the poster, was released in 1921. On the right is the Eagle Tavern, demolished by a V2 in March 1945. The sign on the shop front, left, reads 'City and West End Shirt and Collardressing Company, Receiving Office'.

Raw rubber imported from Malaya being examined at the London Docks. The lifebuoy hanging on the wall has the name Bull Wharf printed on it. Plantation House, the huge Rubber Exchange in Fenchurch Street, built in 1935, where the buying and selling of this commodity was carried out, miraculously survived the Blitz.

Banner displayed at Northumberland Wharf, Preston's Road, on the occasion of the King's trip down the Thames when he opened the King George V Docks on 8 July 1921. The banner reads 'Poplar's message to the King, work or maintenance for the unemployed'.

Seafarers at Limehouse, January 1932. Lascars or Indian seamen were a familiar sight in East London as they came off their ships in search of lodgings. Recruited by the East India Company for their trading vessels, the practice continued through to the shipping lines and steam shipping.

West India Docks, *c.* 1920. A fine view of the sugar warehouses on the north quay. The warehouses were designed by George Gwilt and his son, also George, in 1802. Only a third of the warehouses survived the devastation of the Blitz and they are the finest surviving examples of early nineteenth-century dock architecture. They are now being converted into a leisure complex which will also house the Museum in Docklands.

Seafarers outside a tobacconist's shop,
Limehouse, 1932. Although life on board ship
was harsh and spartan, prospective sailors from
the Calcutta hinterland were eager to earn
their living as lascars. P & O captains found
that 'Asians make useful and accomplished
seamen, they are respectful and obedient, and
if well fed, they can keep the ship in excellent
condition'. They were also paid only a fifth of
their British counterparts' wages.

Burmese restaurant, 78 West India Dock Road, Limehouse, 1932. Little is known about this
establishment, although Philip and Martha Solomon and their six children lived at no. 78 for several years
during the 1930s.

Sherry barrels at London Docks, 1961. These barrels are part of a shipment of sherry, representing over 600,000 bottles; they are being sorted prior to Customs inspection. The Port of London received over two-thirds of the total wines and spirits imported into the United Kingdom each year.

Dunbar's Wharf, Narrow Street, *c.* 1900. At this time it was owned by F.V. Smythe & Co. Note how goods were hoisted directly from carts in the street through the loopholes and into store. They would then be hoisted out at the back of the warehouse into lighters or ships in Limekiln Dock. The wharf was originally owned by Duncan Dunbar, who settled in Limehouse in 1780 and lived in the house on the left, now 138 Narrow Street. His son, also Duncan Dunbar, built Hawrah House in East India Dock Road.

Loading an elephant at the docks, 1882. Jumbo, an African elephant, was sent from Regent's Park to his new owners in America. He was placed in a wooden crate which was hauled by a team of dray-horses to St Katharine's Docks, where it was hoisted by a steam-crane on to a barge which conveyed it down the river to Millwall, where it was transferred to the steam ship *Assyrian Monarch*. The process took three days and was attended by great crowds and several dignitaries, including an American known as 'Elephant Bill' Newman, who was escorting Jumbo to New York.

By the Strangers Home, West India Dock Road, 1926, seafarers fresh off their ships come in search of lodgings. In the 1850s grave concern was expressed about the plight of Asian seamen or lascars, recruited to crew ships from the Far East, only to be discharged and left to fend for themselves in the streets of Poplar. Henry Venn launched an appeal for funds, and in June 1857 the Strangers Home for Asiatics, Africans and South Sea Islanders opened its doors. The vacant Home was used to house families during the slum clearances in 1938, and the present building on this site was opened in November 1946 by Prime Minister Clement Attlee.

The interior of the vaults at London Docks, 1961, showing the storage of rum casks. Wines and spirits occupied a storage space of almost 650,000 sq. ft, yet this was only part of the vast range of warehouses and vaults used for storing goods imported into the Port of London.

Vaults at London Docks, 1890. The vaults were bonded warehouses under the strict control of HM Customs.

Mr Van Loo addresses a meeting of dockers in Victoria Park on 19 June 1948, when 17,000 dockers went on strike. In the distance is the drinking fountain presented to the park by the Victorian philanthropist, Baroness Angela Burdett-Coutts.

Dockers at a meeting in West India Dock Road, 1950. The old Blackwall Railway from Fenchurch Street to Brunswick Pier had long since ceased to function, but was refurbished and now carries the Docklands Light Railway. This view has altered considerably since the highway construction of the Limehouse Link.

Pepper Warehouse Gateway at Leamouth Road, Blackwall, 1935, when it was the property of the LNE Railway. Originally the warehouse was the property of the East India Company, and served as a storehouse for spices. The ruins of the gateway with its distinctive emblem on each pillar survived until it was demolished when the area was being cleared for the construction of the Limehouse Link. A replica has since been put in its place.

Sale of tusks at the London Docks, 1890. The Ivory Warehouse often stored over 10,000 elephant tusks, some of them weighing more than 200 lb, and was the centre of the world's supply of ivory. Tusks varied in colour from pale yellow to dark brown. Also in store were small tusks from whales and teeth from hippopotami and walruses. Hale & Son, Colonial Brokers of 10 Fenchurch Avenue EC, have their names on some of the lots up for auction.

TRADING PLACES

Fruit seller outside the Freemason's Arms, c. 1910. The pub at 96–8 Salmon Lane is still in business.

Horse-drawn delivery van from Wickhams in the Mile End Road, *c.* 1930. The drapery store of Messrs T. Wickhams & Sons was built in 1927 in a style reminiscent of Selfridges. It was built in two sections, because Mr Spiegelhalter, the jeweller at no. 81, refused to sell his site. Wickhams closed in 1969 and it is now a DIY store. The photographer was J. Joseph of Adelina Grove, Stepney.

Poplar Borough Council's horse-drawn dust cart, 1929. Horse carts and horses were a familiar sight in the East End of London well into the 1950s. The dustman is wearing a leather apron and the jackets of both men have leather patches on the shoulders for protection. The men also wore leather trousers, with narrow straps tied below the knees..

The corner of Harford Street, Stepney, 1938. Milly's cosmetics and lingerie was at 412 Mile End Road.

The premises of William Haupt, baker, at 58 Burdett Road, west side, viewed from the north, 1911. No. 60 was occupied by Harris Dworski, butcher. These shops were demolished to form part of King George's Fields, now Mile End Park, opened by the Duke of Edinburgh on 20 October 1952.

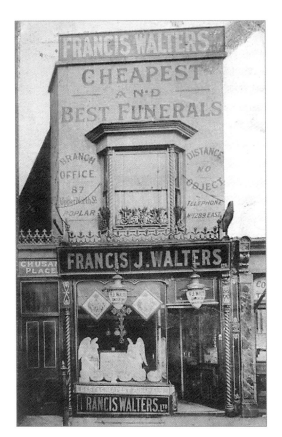

Francis J. Walters' funeral parlour, 811 Commercial Road, Limehouse. The card is dated 3 August 1910, and was sent by Francis Walters to a prospective customer. The establishment, now known as Francis & C.J. Walters, is still in business on the same site, looking very much the same. It was recently refurbished with the help of English Heritage.

The premises of Harry Abrahams, greengrocer, 809 Commercial Road, 15 December 1936. The lamp-post still survives, as does Francis & C. Walters, undertakers, and the pub just visible in the background, the Star of the East. The no. 23 bus route was discontinued in the mid-1980s.

The Black Boy public house, 169 Mile End Road, *c.* 1900. The landlord from 1894 to 1895 was Mr A. Toye, and the Black Boy survived until 1985, when it became the Fifth Avenue Social Club which has since closed. 'Our Joe', 'The Original Our Joe Tobacconist', was Joseph Lyons. The wooden houses were demolished in about 1900 by the Whitechapel & Bow Railway Company and Stepney Green station now stands near the site.

Israel Rosenberg's shop at 220 St George Street, later the Highway, St George's in the East. The shop was next door to Jamrach's Wild Animal Dealers. Rosenberg's son and daughter are standing in the doorway of the shop which has a fascinating array of advertisements.

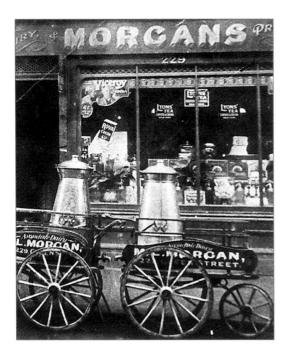

Morgan's dairy and provisions shop at 229
Green Street, now Roman Road, *c*. 1920.

Jones Brothers' bicycle shop at 460–2 Mile End Road, 1937. Mrs Susan Spencer, florist, was at no. 458,
and at no. 464 David Rogers ran his refreshment rooms.

A Chinese restaurant in Limehouse, 1932. No. 60 Pennyfields was the Low Hong Kong Dining Rooms. Here, live chickens are looked over and selected from the barrow for the evening menu. The Chinese settled in Pennyfields around the turn of the century, although their numbers were never very large. In 1918 there were 182 Chinese men living in Pennyfields, of whom 9 were married to English women.

No. 48 Poplar High Street was home to Chee Kong Tong, the Chinese Freemason Society. On 23 May 1931 Fu Chai, aged 38, Secretary of the Chinese Freemasons' Lodge, married Lena Blair, a restaurant counter hand, in the Register Office at Gough Grove. A number of marriages between Chinese merchant seamen and English women took place in Limehouse.

Black Horse public house, 168 Mile End Road, just a few doors eastwards from Hayfield Passage. The landlord, H.S. Kingsley, poses in the doorway with friends to be photographed by the London Commercial Photographic Co. Ltd. The pub's frontage has changed considerably, and is now plainer, and was still trading till recently.

Abraham Cohen's hairdressers and barber's shop at 71 Ellen Street, Stepney. Cohen's was in business between 1923 and 1932.

Lloyd's Steam Laundry, *c.* 1910. The inscription on the window states 'Works 338 Mile End Road'. They had four branches by 1908 after more than a decade of trading there. The picture is undated but the women's attire suggests it is probably early twentieth century.

Commercial Street, 1936. This picture is inscribed with the words: 'This photograph was taken by me at No. 6 Commercial Street on the 31st day of July 1936', and it is signed Charles Thomas Frederick Fowle. Levine's sign announces the sale of coronation decorations.

Blacksmith working at the forge, September 1954, photographed by Halifax Photo Studio of 618 Mile End Road. The smithy was at 10 Claredale Street. The photographer, Halifax Jacobs, the son of Louisa and Harry Jacobs of Jacobs' Garages in Mile End Road, was a flamboyant character who set up a chain of studios around the East End. He was for a time the official photographer of the *East London Advertiser*, and shared the premises in Mile End Road, by the canal, with the newspaper.

Vanhears Coffee Rooms, 564 Commercial Road. Pencilled on the reverse of the picture are the words, 'Went to London on May 12. Returned on June 2nd 1913.' Pictured are the proprietor, Edwin Charles Vanhear, his wife and daughter, and two maids. The coffee rooms were next door to Brothertons, wireworkers, still in business.

Casting guns at the Munitions Foundry, Commercial Gas Company, 1915–17. Here molten metal is being poured into the wooden cases, inside each of which is a mould for half of the gun case. Soot and sand were used to settle the molten metal and so form the gun case.

Man standing in the doorway of a Chinese grocery store in Limehouse Causeway, 1930. The entire area was cleared in the late 1930s as part of Stepney's slum clearance project, and the Causeway was widened, resulting in the disappearance of what had become known as Chinatown in Limehouse.

THE GREAT AND THE GOOD

The Virginia Settlers Memorial at Blackwall, 1951. The second memorial to be placed at Blackwall, it was erected to commemorate the journey of the three little ships and 105 men who embarked from this spot and sailed across the Atlantic to become the first permanent settlers in Virginia, USA. The sculpture of a mermaid was the work of Harold Brown and was placed on a plinth created from granite stones taken from the West India Dock Gates. The memorial was unveiled on 18 May 1951 by the American Ambassador, in the presence of the Bishop of London and representatives of the Association for the Preservation of Virginia Antiquities. Both bronze statue and plaque were subsequently stolen and in 1971 a new plaque was placed on the plinth after the building of the Brunswick Power Station. This plaque has since been removed and is in the custody of the Museum in Docklands.

Dr Barnardo and his daughter Queenie. Born in July 1879 in the Bow Road, and christened Gwendoline Maud Syrie, Queenie was the daughter of Dr Thomas and Syrie Barnardo. Barnardo was a very strict father in the true Victorian mould, and Queenie's attempts to escape his authority by marrying the elderly Henry Wellcome, twenty-five years her senior, led to even further unhappiness when her son was taken away from her and given to foster-parents. Queenie later married W. Somerset Maugham, by whom she had a daughter, Liza, but the marriage ended in further unhappiness and acrimony.

Mrs Syrie Barnardo, 1910. Born Syrie Emslie in 1848, she married Dr Thomas Barnardo in June 1873, and came to live in East London to join him in his work. She set up and organised the Deaconesses Home at 32 Bow Road, and later ran the Servant Girls Registry, where young East End girls were trained for domestic work. After her husband's death in 1905, Syrie Barnardo lived with her daughter Queenie. She died, aged 96, in December 1944 and was interred with her husband at Barkingside.

Dr Barnardo's coffin at the People's Mission Church, Edinburgh Castle, where it was on view from 23 to 27 September 1905. Dr Thomas Barnardo founded his East End Juvenile Mission in 1868 in Hope Place, Limehouse. He went on to set up homes and schools for destitute children, one of his institutions being the Ragged School in Copperfield Road. He took over the notorious Edinburgh Castle and turned it into a Mission. Barnardo is buried in Barkingside, where a memorial commemorates his life and work.

Bernard Bresslaw (1934–93) meets his fans at the Odeon Cinema in Mile End Road, October 1960, at the mobile unit X-ray campaign. The actor was born in Stepney in 1934, lived in Eric Street and attended the Cooper's School from where he won a scholarship to study drama at the Royal Academy of Dramatic Art. A versatile actor, well known from the 'Carry On' films, he was equally at home on the Shakespearean stage.

John William Burrows, Beadle, in 1863. Burrows is believed to have been the last Beadle of the parish of
Bethnal Green; he was a great character, whose nose was described as a 'grog blossom', but he looked so
resplendent in his official dress that during the visit of Queen Victoria on 2 April 1873 he was mistaken
for the First Commissioner of Works. He lived at Ivy Cottage in Mowlem Street, just off Bishops Way,
and was often seen riding about in his pony chaise.

Ann Tago Bryant, née Carkeet (1804–79), was the wife of William Bryant, whom she married in 1833. In July 1861 Bryant and his partner Francis May opened the Bryant & May Match Factory in Fairfield Road, Bow. Ann and William's son Wilberforce turned the business into a public company in 1884, and four years later the high profits earned by the shareholders and the wretched working conditions in the factory inspired Annie Besant to lead the match-girls out on an historic strike.

William Whiffin (1878–1957) was born in Poplar, the son of W.H. Whiffin, photographer. Together with his father and brother Ernest, William Whiffin opened a photographic studio at 237 East India Dock Road. It is largely thanks to him that Poplar has such an extensive and well-documented photographic archive. Whiffin presented a collection of pictures to the London Museum, as well as Bancroft Library, though his own collection was ruined when his studio was damaged by the V2 rocket which destroyed the Eagle pub in March 1945.

Robert Wild, President of the National Union of Teachers, 1885. The headmaster of St Michael's Schools, Poplar, Robert Wild remained in his post from 1862 until his retirement in 1906. During his tenure the school changed its name to Byron Street in 1878 under the London School Board. In 1908 the London County Council renamed it the Hay Currie School. Wild was well known locally and nationally for his work with the National Union of Teachers and was an opponent of the system of payment by results which was abolished in the 1890s.

Dr Hannah Billig with her patient Maurice Woolf, aged 12, 1960. Hannah Billig was born in Hanbury Street in 1901, the third child of Barnet and Millie Billig, Jewish refugees. She went on to excel at school, qualified as a doctor, and set up her surgery at 198 Cable Street, Stepney. Dr Billig was awarded the George Medal in 1941 for her bravery during the Blitz; after serving as a army doctor in India she was made an MBE. She returned to her Cable Street practice, and continued serving her patients until her retirement in 1964. Dr Billig settled in Caesaria, Israel, where she died in 1987.

Jack Warner, 'Dixon of Dock Green', was born Horace John Waters in 1895 at 1 Rounton Road, Bow. As a lad he played the viola in the family orchestra. His sisters Elsie and Doris played the violin and piano. Jack Warner made a name for himself during the Second World War in the BBC's Garrison Theatre series.

The Beverley Sisters, Teddy, Joy and Babs, May 1951. The famous singing trio are the daughters of George and Victoria Coram, who were a cross-talk comedy team known as Coram and Mills. George Coram had a furniture shop in Devon's Road, Bromley-by-Bow, where the family lived.

Annie Barnes, 1916. Born in Stepney in 1887, the eldest daughter of a fruiterer who had a large shop near Burdett Road, Annie went to Ben Jonson School and later joined the Suffragettes under the leadership of Sylvia Pankhurst. As a member of the Labour Party in Stepney, Annie canvassed for Clement Attlee in Limehouse, and was herself elected to Stepney Council in 1934, besides working in the community to redress social injustice. Annie Barnes died in early 1982.

Prince Ras Monolulu in Club Row, 1936. Probably the best-known racing tipster in England, he paraded through the Petticoat Lane area dressed in baggy trousers and a head-dress of ostrich feathers, with a furled umbrella, cajoling prospective customers with his familiar cry of 'I gotta horse'. Prince Monolulu was in fact a Maori named Peter McKay who came to this country at the turn of the century. He died in 1965 when he was well into his eighties.

Phil Kay with Prince Monolulu in Fieldgate Street, 11 November 1936. Phil Kay, who changed his surname from Kalisky to Kay in 1920, started work at the Sack and Bag Factory in Shadwell owned by his father, Michael Kalisky, and was a union activist. During the First World War the firm prospered, reclaiming sacks for military use. Kay later ran his own business, the Limehouse Sack Works Ltd at 134 St Paul's Way, which supplied sacks for sandbags and other military uses during the Second World War.

Poet and painter Isaac Rosenberg (seated) with his brother Elkon, photographed in September 1917 when they were on leave in London. Isaac Rosenberg's talent was encouraged first by his headmaster at the Baker Street School, Stepney, and later by the librarian at Whitechapel Library. He went on to study at the Slade School of Fine Art, while continuing to write poetry. Isaac Rosenberg joined the army in October 1915 and was killed in action on 1 April 1918.

No. 87 Dempsey Street (the house with the light door), Stepney, home of Isaac Rosenberg. His parents were Lithuanian refugees and he was one of five children. This photograph was taken in 1960. The houses have since been demolished.

Thomas Jackson's funeral procession, Mile End Road, 1930. In 1906 Jackson purchased the old Congregational Chapel, the Brunswick Hall, and set up the Whitechapel Mission. He was a pioneer in rehabilitation work with young offenders, which paved the way for the Probation Service. Jackson helped to found the Garment Workers' Union and was a campaigner against the practice of 'sweating' – the exploitation of homeworkers. The Mission he founded became a refuge for the homeless, work that is still carried on today.

Queen Alexandra's statue in the gardens of the London Hospital at Whitechapel. The statue commemorates the first introduction into England of the Finsen light treatment for leprosy and other diseases. The Queen was the patron of the hospital and took a great interest in its work, visiting it on a number of occasions. The hospital was renamed the Royal London Hospitals NHS Trust in 1991.

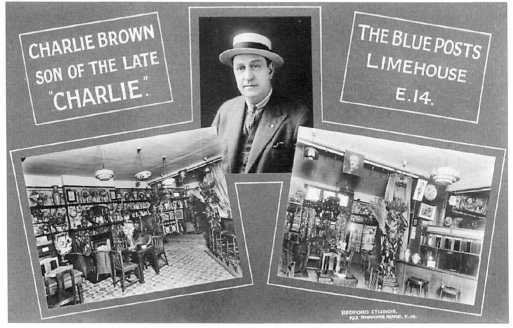

Charlie Brown, landlord of the Blue Posts, West India Dock Road, Limehouse, 1934. Charlie was the son of the famous Charlie Brown, who owned the Railway Tavern, just opposite the Blue Posts, in West India Dock Road. The interior view on the right of the picture includes Charlie senior's portrait, along with many of the antiques and curios which had made his pub so famous.

WAR AND THE AFTERMATH

Collecting scrap for the war effort at Northumberland Wharf, Blackwall, c. 1940. St Nicholas's Church can be seen in the background. The church was bombed during the war and subsequently demolished. The site of this yard and the church now form part of the Tower Hamlets Waste Reclamation Depot. Blackwall Buildings can be seen on the left.

St Barnabas Church in Grove Road, on the corner with Roman Road, 1944, showing the effects of bomb damage. The church was restored, but is now minus its spire, which appeared to have survived the bombing. Nos 336–8 Roman Road on the right used to be the premises of Barclays Bank. These buildings were demolished and the area is now a park.

George Lansbury, who led the Labour councillors to victory in the first post-war elections, takes a turn on the roundabout at the Old English Fair in Poplar Park, August 1919.

Peace party for children in Culloden Street, Bromley-by-Bow, 1919, photographed by William Whiffin.

Hall Street Peace Party, 1919. Grace Gibson, seen wearing a sailor suit, was twenty-two years old and living in Hall Street, Poplar, when this picture was taken. During the war Grace worked as a cutter and dryer in a tobacco manufacturers in Aldgate. She recalled that her wages were 26s 6d a week, but after the war she was moved, along with the other women, to the packing department where they earned between 15 and 17s a week.

Local people watch a service being held at the site of the Single Street School in Stepney, 15 September 1942, the second anniversary of the Battle of Britain. The service was attended by the mayors of the local boroughs, as well as men of the RAF, Civil Defence workers and nurses.

A contingent of the Royal Navy pulling cannon along Commercial Road in the Peace Day Parade, 1936. To the left is Timothy White's household store at 583 Commercial Road.

Sophie Tucker, the American jazz singer, makes a special appearance at the Rivoli Theatre, August 1921. The Rivoli was opened on Monday 1 August on the site of the old Wonderland, and was considered the last word in luxury. During the first week of opening the programme featured W.S. Hart in *Sand*, *The Mutiny of Elsinore*, *A Yankee at the Court of King Arthur* and *Carmen*. There was also the additional attraction of a variety programme.

The Rivoli Theatre, November 1961. Severely damaged during the Second World War, it remained an empty shell for twenty years before being demolished. The Citroën Garage was built on part of the site, along with the East London Mosque, constructed in 1985.

Slipping the Slip in Poplar Recreation Ground, September 1919, when the English Fair was held to celebrate the end of the First World War.

Ernest Street, Stepney, from Harford Street, looking west, 1941. The street suffered severe bomb damage and many houses, as well as the Latimer Congregational Chapel, were destroyed. The church was rebuilt as a modern, functional building, and the church hall is used as a lecture room by the East London History Society.

Tower Hill after an air raid. On the right are the ruined offices of Murray & Laker, shipping and custom house agents and licensed car-men at nos 26–7. The photographer has noted the time of his picture very precisely as '12.35 p.m. 9th December 1940'. The construction of the Port of London Authority headquarters in Trinity Square, seen towering in the background, began in 1912 and was completed in 1922.

The ruins of St Stephen's Church in Poplar, May 1945. The church was consecrated in 1867 and was a landmark along the East India Dock Road until its destruction by a rocket which landed beside it in November 1944. The rocket also demolished houses in three adjoining streets, killing five people. The site was cleared for the Festival of Britain's showpiece architecture, the Lansbury Estate, in 1951.

The landlord and his wife at the door of the Royal Oak public house, Cayley Street, 1 October 1947. Appearances are deceptive, as the picture on the right shows.

The rear of the Royal Oak pub showing the ruined walls. All the housing in this area was demolished and it has been turned into a playground.

Trinity Congregational Chapel, East India Dock Road, lies in ruins following an air raid on 3 August 1944. In the background can be seen the Queen Victoria Seamen's Rest, also extensively damaged. The Emery Hall in the background appears unscathed. Part of the Seamen's Mission buildings, the Emery Hall is now being used as a community theatre.

Air-raid shelter in the boiler house of the Poplar Methodist Mission. Whiling away the time playing cards are Mr Walker, Revd I. Morgan, Mrs Walker, Mr W. Carey and Mr J. Pearce.

Whitechapel Baths, Goulston Street, showing bomb damage, 3 March 1945. The baths and wash-house were opened in 1846, before the first Act of Parliament enabling authorities to establish them; closed in 1858 the baths were refurbished before reopening in 1878. There were three swimming baths here, first and second class men's and ladies' baths and a marble bath. The baths closed in 1990.

Bethnal Green Underground station shelter, December 1943. People sheltering from the air raids are treated to a New Year's Eve Concert. Only a few months earlier, on 3 March 1943, the worst civilian disaster of the war occurred here, when 173 men, women and children were killed in a stampede on the stairs.

The ruins of the Dissenters Mortuary Chapel in Tower Hamlets Cemetery, 1966. The chapel, one of two built, stood in the south-east corner of the cemetery. The octagonal-shaped chapel was designed by architects Wyatt and Brandon in the Byzantine style. Surmounted by a lantern, with twin arches in each segment and a porch at one side, it also had extensive catacombs for single coffins or family vaults. Built in 1849 by the Cemetery Company, the chapel was damaged during the Second World War and demolished by the GLC in 1972.

St George's Hospital was damaged by aerial bombardment on 11 March 1941. The hospital stood near the end of Wapping Lane, and in 1955 it was converted into a home for refugees.

Granary fire at the Three Mills Distillery in July 1920. The *East End News* of 29 July reported that on the Sunday morning at half-past four, the distillery of Messrs J.W. Nicholson & Co. of Bromley caught fire. The blaze had started in the four-storey granary building, spreading to the other buildings before the fire brigade could get it under control. Much of the 5,000–6,000 quarters of grain stored in the building was destroyed, but the fire was eventually brought under control before it spread to the whisky tanks.

St Paul's Church, Bow Common, viewed from Burdett Road, 1950. The pre-fab houses were on the east side, between Turners Road and St Paul's Way. Although pre-fabs were intended to be a temporary replacement, some of them lasted well into the 1990s, the last ones in Poplar being demolished in 1996.

Bethnal Green Tube shelter library, 1942. The opening hours for the lending library were 5.30 to 8 p.m. on working days. A notice on the door states 'Raid in Progress', presumably meaning that the staff were not available to serve, but perhaps the daring photographer just had to take a quick picture!

A royal visit to East India Dock Road, 9 May 1945. King George VI and Queen Elizabeth, with the two princesses, at the site of the Eagle public house on the corner of Cotton Street. A V2 rocket exploded here at 11.50 a.m. on 7 March, killing 20 people and injuring a further 120, many of whom had been standing at the bus stop outside All Saints' Church. The Queen is speaking to Mrs Margetts, Post Warden, while the King chats to Mr A. Cole, District Warden. The photograph was taken by William Whiffin.

Remembrance Day, observed on Sunday 10 November 1957. The British Legion honours those who gave their lives in the defence of their country. This photograph is by Halifax Studios.

The railway arch over Bethnal Green Road, looking west from Cambridge Heath Road, pictured during Bethnal Green Warship Week, 21–8 March 1942. The Salmon and Ball pub, on the extreme left of the picture, has its origins in the eighteenth century. A sign on the bridge reads: 'The oldest Inn in the district

— 300 yards on right'. This refers to the Old George at 379 Bethnal Green Road, mentioned in Messrs Truman, Hanbury and Buxton's account book of 1742. Rebuilt in 1879, it survived until about 1990.

Festival of Britain crane, 1951. Erected on the site of the Architecture, Town-planning and Building Research Exhibition in Poplar, at 200 ft high it was the tallest crane ever made in Britain. It stood on the corner of East India Dock Road and Upper North Street, just opposite the site of St Stephen's Church.

THE CHURCH AND ITS PEOPLE

Fr Joe Williamson in Fletcher Street, December 1962, shortly before his retirement. Born in Arcadia Street, Poplar, in 1895 to a working-class family, Joseph Williamson aspired to the priesthood from an early age. In 1952 Father Joe was sent to St Paul's in Dock Street, where he quickly became involved in combating the social problems of poor housing and homelessness in the Cable Street area.

The Bishop of Stepney pictured at a garden fête in aid of the Combined Hospitals Appeal, Poplar Park, 21 July 1922. The event was opened by the Countess of Buxton, seen here with the Bishop and George Lansbury.

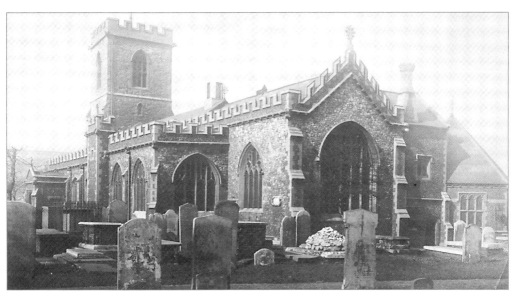

St Dunstan's Church, 1890. The old church of St Dunstan stands in a 7-acre churchyard and is the oldest building in Tower Hamlets. A Saxon church stood here during Domesday times. It may originally have been called All Hallows, later being renamed after Dunstan, the Bishop of London who died in AD 988, and was placed in the Calendar of Saints by King Canute in 1029. The main rebuilding took place c. 1500, but only fragments of the original building are visible. The tower of the church once had a beacon, which was lighted at night to guide wayfarers in the countryside around.

St Dunstan's Church interior, 1890. The church has a Saxon rood, a stone slab about 39 by 27 inches, carved with the Saviour on the Cross and the Virgin Mary and St John below. There is also another carving of the Annunciation, thought to date from the fourteenth century. On the north side of the altar is the tomb of Sir Henry Colet, the wealthy merchant who belonged to the Mercers' Company and was twice Lord Mayor of London. Many other eminent mariners and sea captains are also buried in St Dunstan's. The vestry men of St Dunstan's were drawn from merchants, gentry and sea captains.

Zoar Chapel pulpit. This photograph was taken in February 1915 and shows the pulpit and staircase of the
Zoar Chapel, which was in Great Alie Street, Whitechapel. The label on the underside of the pulpit had
the date 1750, although its style would suggest an earlier period.

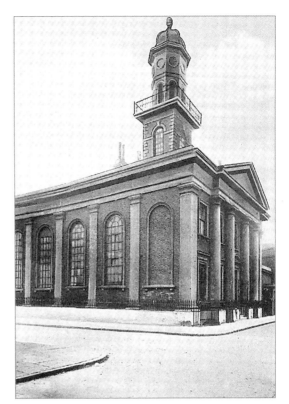

The Church of Our Lady and St Casimir, the
Polish Catholic Church, Mercer Street, on the
corner of what is now Shadwell Street and
Juniper Street, Shadwell. Originally the
London Sailors' Institute, built by the British
and Foreign Sailors' Society and opened on 23
July 1856, it was the headquarters of the
Society and became the model for institutes the
world over. It had a reading room, library,
lecture room and temperance bar, classrooms
and a savings bank, and it served seafarers for
almost fifty years.

View of the ornate altar in the Church of Our Lady and St Casimir. The church was opened in 1905 in the
former London Sailors' Institute, but was later used as the premises of a tarpaulin manufacturers until the
1960s when the building was demolished. The site is now occupied by Blue Gate Fields School.

St Paul's Church and Sailors Home, Dock Street, Stepney. The foundation stone for this church was laid on 11 May 1846 by Prince Albert, who also presented a set of communion plate to the church. St Paul's was built to replace the floating church *Brazen*, which was moored in the Pool of London. The architect was H. Roberts and the church was designed in the Early English style and built at a cost of £9,000. The spire was surmounted by a weather-vane in the form of a ship. In 1859 the minister in charge was the Revd Daniel Greatorex, the Sailors' Chaplain, remembered in the name Greatorex Street in Whitechapel. Another famous vicar was the Revd Joe Williamson.

The Crystal Tavern on the corner of Bridge Street, *c.* 1900. The pub operated until 1996, and is presently undergoing refurbishment. The Baptist Tabernacle, which was built in about 1870 and could seat 2,000 people, can be seen in the background. Bridge Street is now Hamlets Way, and leads to Tower Hamlets Cemetery Park.

Interior of Trinity Congregational Church, East India Dock Road, 14 December 1909. The church was built by George Green, shipbuilder and philanthropist of Poplar, who did not approve of the high Anglican church decor at All Saints'. The church was completely destroyed on 3 August 1944 but was rebuilt in time to be an architectural showpiece for the Festival of Britain in 1951.

Trinity Congregational Chapel, East India Dock Road, 1930. It is now the Trinity Methodist Church.

St Matthias's Church, Poplar, under a blanket of snow, 1935. The view is from the south-west, showing the monument of Captain Samuel Jones. The church was built by the East India Company in 1654 as a chapel, and was refurbished in 1776 and 1876, when the clock-tower was added and the brick chapel encased in Kentish ragstone. Since its closure in the 1970s the church has been restored and is now a community centre and the Island History Trust's new base.

A Chinese funeral taking place at East London Cemetery, 1922. The Chinese mourners are wearing Tong collars. The Chinese Freemasons' Society was at 48 Pennyfields. The interment is observed by a Rabbi,' although the deceased was not of the Jewish faith. He was there because the law required 'an accredited minister' to officiate at an interment.

Revd Morris Roberts with his pet cockatoo, *c.* 1920. The Revd Roberts was vicar of St Matthias's Church in Poplar from 1899 until his death in September 1925.

Alfred Yeo, MP for Poplar, with the Revd William Lax, enjoys a ride on a swing at the Old English Fayre in Poplar Recreation Ground, August 1919.

Opening the new 'Tab' in Zetland Street, Bromley-by-Bow, Saturday 6 January 1951. A modest construction, the Poplar and Berger Baptist Tabernacle was rebuilt on the site of the old 'Tab' to replace Berger Hall in Empson Street, destroyed on the first night of the Blitz, and the Poplar and Bromley Tabernacle which suffered the same fate in March 1941. The minister was the Revd Lionel Jupp.

Revd Alfred Tildsley and Mrs Tildsley. The Revd Tildsley was minister at the Poplar and Bromley Tabernacle in Bromley-by-Bow for forty-seven years. He is credited with being the first person to show magic lantern slides in a church. He went on to found the film corporation that later became Paramount Pictures. Alfred Tildsley died on 3 January 1949, surviving his wife by a year.

Ernest Bartlett (1870–1942), seen here as a young man with his family. Bartlett was born in Bow, but spent all his life in Bethnal Green. Educated at the Olga Street School, he worked in a marine insurance office. He was a keen collector of prints and other material relating to Bethnal Green, and was for many years associated with St Barnabas Church, Roman Road.

The Ladies' Institute of the Congregational Chapel at Bruce Road, Bromley-by-Bow, *c.* 1910. The group is seated in the park behind the chapel, but the identities of the ladies and gentlemen have yet to be discovered.

Canon Bartholomew O'Doherty pictured in the presbytery gardens in 1930. Canon O'Doherty was parish priest at St Mary and St Joseph's RC Church, Poplar, from 1921 to 1945, and he was in the presbytery when a landmine demolished the church on 8 December 1940. He died in August 1950.

Mile End Road, looking towards the north-east, and the clock-tower of the People's Palace and St Benet's Church, 1899. The church, a large building of dull red brick, was built in 1870 and endowed out of funds derived from the sale of St Benet's Church in Gracechurch Street. A modern chapel was built on the site after the war.

The procession of the Blessed Sacrament through the parish of St Mary's and St Michael's Church, Commercial Road, 1964. Shrines outside Catholic homes were not uncommon and the parish priest would halt the procession and bless the shrine as the faithful passed through the neighbourhood. The church was built in 1856 to replace the Virginia Street Chapel, which the congregation of largely Irish Catholics had outgrown.

Corpus Christi procession, St Mary's and St Michael's Church, 1964. Monsignor Derek Worlock was the rector in 1964, and Father Patrick Casey was the parish priest.

The interior of Christ Church, Watney Street, after war damage. The church had one of the finest interiors in East London. It was built by James Weddell Bridger, and designed by architect James Shaw in the Romanesque style, of grey bricks with stone dressings. Consecrated on 3 May 1844, Christ Church served one of the most deprived areas of Stepney, where one in fourteen of the population were paupers.

Christ Church, Watney Street, 1943, showing the extensive damage caused by a landmine on 16 April 1941. The Revd William Quekett was the first vicar, and served until 1854. In 1847 Quekett helped to collate statistics of the area, and was to find that there were no fewer than fifty brothels in the vicinity of the church! Quekett went on to set up three schools, plus a ragged school for the very poor, and eventually another church. The site was built over in 1967, and forms part of the Watney Market complex, roughly where the supermarket now stands.

St John's Church in Scandrett Street, Wapping, 1936. All that remains of this church is the tower, although the Charity School on the right, now converted into apartments, has survived, as have the wooden painted charity girl and boy standing in their twin alcoves above the main entrance. The church was built in 1755–60 by Joel Johnson, replacing the earlier chapel built in 1617.

St Peter's Church in Old Gravel Lane, Wapping, July 1938. A year later Old Gravel Lane was renamed Wapping Lane. The church was built in 1859 and opened in 1865. The Revd Charles Lowder was its first charismatic vicar, whose good work was continued by another well-loved priest, Father Wainwright. The church, now St Peter's with St John's, was restored in 1956. It is approached through an arch, which partly hides it from the view of the passer-by. The east window of the chapel was one of the early works of Burne-Jones.

The Ferrers monument in the north aisle of St Leonard's Church, Bromley-by-Bow. Dating to 1625, the memorial bears the inscription 'Live well and dye never, Dye well and live ever'. The church was formerly the Benedictine Chapel of St Mary of the Priory of St Leonard's, and was rebuilt several times. It was one of the casualties of the Second World War.

St Stephen's Vicarage lawn, Wednesday 14 June 1911, a Mothers' and Fathers' Tea Party to celebrate the coronation of King George V and Queen Mary. The vicar was the Revd H.A. Mason, and by East End standards the guests appear to be fairly affluent. Centre background is a stage, to the left of which an orchestra is playing. The church in Bow was one of the casualties of the Second World War.

ACKNOWLEDGEMENTS

Many of the photographs we have selected are from the Whiffin Collection in Tower Hamlets Local History Library. We are grateful to the Local History Library for making available their extensive collection of photographs, many of which have been donated to the Library.

Acknowledgements are due also to the following: Mr A.G. Ayres, ATV Photo Information, Mr A. Bazzone, Frederick Bennett, Central Press Agency, *Daily Mirror*, *Daily Telegraph*, J. Dixon-Scott, Dr Barnardo's, Fox Photos, Mrs Grace Gibson, Halifax Photos, Holland and Hannen and Cubitt Ltd, Island History Trust, Keystone Press, Ernie Johnson, London Metropolitan Archives, Gladys Manister (née Whiffin), Museum in Docklands, PA-Reuters, Mrs Page, *Planet News*, Poplar Methodist Mission, Port of London Authority, Pritchard Photo Co., Maurice Rickards, Royal Commission on Historical Monuments (England), Mr P. Sanders, Salvation Army International Heritage Centre, Mr E.W. Taylor, Mr W. Turner, Sam Vincent, Renee Weller, John Walker, Mr K. Wheelan, Whitechapel Mission, Miss Rose Woolf.

Our thanks go also to Philip Mernick for contributions from his extensive postcard collection.